This book belongs to:

....

Notes for Parents

- Encourage your child to find the picture stickers and answer the questions in the book.

- Use the gold star stickers to praise their successes, and to encourage their 'green' habits.

- Fill in the 'I will' tasks on the wipe-clean reward chart, and the star targets and rewards. Your child will enjoy joining in with this too, particularly in choosing the rewards. They will love the sense of responsibility, and the excitement of working towards the treats they've chosen.

- Rewards need not be big, but they should be meaningful to your child: an extra bedtime story, baking a cake, going to the swimming pool or the park, having a friend to play, a pocket money treat – something that they enjoy, and that you feel is appropriate to what they have achieved.

- Always keep a positive attitude and remember to focus on their achievements. Never take away stickers or deny a reward that has been agreed and earned.

- Your child will soon appreciate that being 'green' can be fun, and these positive early habits will help to encourage them to grow to be responsible and thoughtful people.

ISBN 978-1-84135-908-3

Copyright © 2012 Award Publications Limited

First published 2012

Published by Award Publications Limited,
The Old Riding School, Welbeck,
Worksop, S80 3LR

18 4

Printed in Malaysia

The Children's Book of GREEN HABITS

Sophie Giles

Illustrated by Kate Davies

AWARD PUBLICATIONS LIMITED

Our use of fossil fuels has polluted our planet. Your impact upon the environment is known as your 'carbon footprint' – the more you pollute, the bigger your carbon footprint is.

How have humans polluted the earth?

By using renewable energy sources we can help protect our planet from pollution. We can each do this every day by trying hard to follow the three R's:
Reduce, **R**euse and **R**ecycle.

I reduce, reuse and recycle

Do you follow the three R's?

Water is vital for our survival. In some places people walk miles to fetch drinking water. In other places, water is wasted

daily. A bath can use up to 80 litres of water, and running the tap whilst cleaning your teeth can waste 3.5 litres! **Why is water so important?**

Taking a shower instead of a bath can save up to 45 litres of water – that's 3 weeks' drinking water for one person! Keeping a jug of water in the fridge saves running the tap each time for cold drinks. **How do you reduce the amount of water you use?**

I save water

Some careless people have left their rubbish behind after a picnic. Attracted by the smell of the leftover food, some animals have become caught in the packaging.

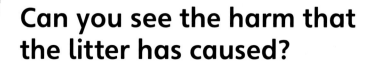

Can you see the harm that the litter has caused?

Remember to take your rubbish home with you. There you can make sure that it is put in the bin or, where possible, recycled. Crush cans and cut up plastics so that wildlife will not be harmed.

Do you take your litter home with you?

I put litter in the bin

Batteries must be disposed of safely and should never be put in the fire. If not properly recycled they can end up in landfill sites where they can poison the environment.

Why should batteries be recycled?

Try to use rechargeable batteries. They can usually be recharged up to 500 times! Or, better still, use solar-powered or wind-up phone chargers, torches and radios. That way you save money and energy!

Do you use renewable energy?

I use renewable energy

Fumes from vehicles pollute the air. They create acid rain that poisons water supplies and plants. Animals can suffer too. They

can become ill and even die because their food and water supply is poisoned by the pollution.

What has killed the fish?

We can reduce our carbon footprint by using public transport or car-sharing on journeys. Whenever you can, try to walk or cycle to places as this creates no emissions and is healthier for you, too!

How can you reduce your carbon footprint?

I reduce my carbon footprint

Oil is used to make plastics, and the factories that make them cause pollution. Plastic items which cannot be recycled are buried in landfill sites and take hundreds of years to rot away.

What fossil fuel is used to make plastic?

Scientists have developed plastics that can be recycled into fuel, and even clothes. To reduce the use of landfill sites, recycle or reuse plastic items. This greenhouse is built from empty drinks bottles.

What plastic items do you recycle?

I recycle plastics

Some trees are grown specially to make paper, but the process still destroys wildlife habitats and creates pollution. If you

 throw away paper instead of recycling it, more trees must be cut down in order to make new paper.

What is paper made from?

You can easily recycle paper products by putting them into the recycling bin. You can even reuse them to make your own paper and create handmade greetings cards.

How else could you reuse paper?

I recycle paper

Unwanted or broken toys are often thrown away. Unfortunately, some waste is burned. When burned, poisonous chemicals in electronic equipment create toxic fumes that pollute the air, causing acid rain.

What damage is caused by acid rain?

Be responsible and consider if you really need new toys. Can your old toys be fixed? Could you swap them with a friend? How else can unwanted toys be recycled?

I am responsible with my toys

Are you a Crazy Consumer or a Sensible Shopper?

Droughts occur when there is not enough rainfall to provide all the water we need. Reservoirs store water, but during droughts they can run low. Plants, animals and crop production can suffer.

When do droughts happen?

You can help to save water by collecting rain to water your garden, instead of using a hosepipe. Some houses have special systems to recycle bath and shower water so it can be reused to flush the toilet.

I recycle water

How could you recycle water?

Although many clothes are made from natural products such as cotton or wool, they do not recycle as easily as paper or food, so care needs to be taken when disposing of them.

Where does wool come from?

Think carefully before you throw away old clothes, could they be mended or reused? You could help others by donating them to a charity shop, or use them as rags for cleaning.

I reuse my old clothes

How else could you make use of your old clothes?

Although renewable energy sources, such as wind turbines and solar power, are becoming more common, most of our electricity still comes from fossil fuels, which pollute the planet.

What gives us solar power?

We can reduce the amount of energy we waste by switching off lights and electrical items when they are not being used. Wear suitable clothing to avoid needing to use the air conditioning or heating.

Do you save energy?

I switch off lights

Aluminium cans may take up to 200 years to rot away. To make new cans, a raw material called bauxite must be mined from the ground. Mines destroy habitats and pollute the air, water and earth.

What is aluminium made from?

Recycled aluminium is not only used to make new cans, but also saucepans, bicycles, car parts, building materials and even aeroplanes!

Where is your local recycling collection point?

I use my local recycling point

Large areas of rainforest have been turned into farms to provide food for the growing population of the world. But 1.3 billion tonnes of food is wasted worldwide each year.

Why is it bad that rainforests are cleared for farming?

Reduce your food waste by planning meals together as a family. Compost bins are a great way to recycle uncooked food waste – and you can use the compost to grow your own vegetables, too.

How could you reduce your food waste?

I save leftover food

Make Your Own Recycled Paper

You will need:

- old picture frame
- nylon tights
- drawing pins
- shredded or torn-up paper (not glossy or shiny paper)
- washing-up bowl
- potato masher
- leaves and/or flower petals
- sponge
- newspaper
- cloths/towels
- rolling pin

Making the Frame

1. Ask an adult to help you remove the glass and backing board from the old picture frame.

2. Cut a piece from the tights the same size as the frame. Stretch the tights material over one side of the frame and hold in place using the drawing pins. Make sure the material is tightly stretched!

Making the Pulp

1. Shred or rip the paper into bits and soak these in warm water for at least one hour.

2. Mash the soaked paper with the potato masher until it looks like thick, lumpy soup.

Make Your Own Recycled Paper

Making the Paper

1. Half fill the bowl with water and add 2 or 3 handfuls of the paper pulp. Add a few leaves or petals. Then swirl the mixture about.

2. With the material-covered side at the bottom, slowly dip the frame into the water. Once completely under the water, move it about gently to fill it evenly with pulp.

3. Keeping the frame flat, lift it straight up and out of the water. Count from one to twenty as you let the water drain back into the bowl.

4. Next, turn the frame over onto the pile of cloths. Carefully press down on the mesh with a sponge to soak up the excess water.

5. Lift and remove the frame.

6. Put a sheet of newspaper on top of the recycled paper and turn the whole pile upside down.

7. Using the rolling pin, squeeze out any excess water from the paper while it is between the cloths and newspaper.

8. Remove the cloths and leave your paper to dry. Finally, gently peel your paper from the newspaper.

 **Pollution** is the name given to any sort of impurity in the environment that causes an imbalance.

Renewable energy is an energy source that can be used again and again, like solar power.

 **Raw materials** are natural resources used or changed to make other products. Wood is the main raw material for paper.

A **habitat** is the natural home of an animal or a plant. For example, a pond is a frog's natural habitat.

 **Fossil fuels** such as coal, oil and gas were formed from decomposed prehistoric plants. Burning fossil fuels creates carbon dioxide emissions.

A **landfill** site, also known as a tip or rubbish dump, is where waste materials are buried and disposed of.